I0804823

IMAGES of America

MANHATTAN BEACH POLICE DEPARTMENT

This map of Manhattan Beach indicates different areas of the community.

IMAGES
of America

MANHATTAN BEACH POLICE DEPARTMENT

Jan Dennis

ARCADIA
PUBLISHING

ISBN 978-0-7385-2089-6

Published by Arcadia Publishing
Charleston, South Carolina

Printed in the United States of America

Library of Congress Catalog Card Number: Applied For.

For all general information contact Arcadia Publishing at:
Telephone 843-853-2070
Fax 843-853-0044
E-Mail sales@arcadiapublishing.com
For customer service and orders:
Toll-Free 1-888-313-2665

Visit us on the Internet at www.arcadiapublishing.com

In its early days Manhattan Beach moved at a very slow pace with very little crime.

Contents

ACKNOWLEDGMENTS

Few projects are accomplished without the help or advice of others. Once again I had the good fortune and privilege of having the assistance, dedication, and interest of John Scott. Without his editorial talent and technical photographic enhancement skills, this book would not have the visual strength and clarity that appears on the following pages. No less appreciation is extended to Esther Besbris, who spent many hours reading and editing the text. In the search for visual material I shall always be indebted to the many residents who generously shared their album photos and memorabilia, bringing the past to life.

A big thank you to Police Chief Ernest Klevesahl, fondly referred to as "Chief Ernie," who gave me the encouragement to produce this history of the Manhattan Beach Police Department and allowed me to work so closely with Sergeant Nan Rados and the department staff.

This acknowledgement would not be complete without expressing my gratitude to police force retirees Steve Fletcher and Fred McKewen whose scrap books and anecdotes lent both photos and text to this publication. Another special thank-you for invaluable help must go to Don Lastra, Bill Matson, former Chief Hugh O'Brian, Bruce Powell, Anita Spikula, Bob Quinlan, and Jack Zea.

Photographs, Books, and Newspaper Credit:

Battman-Corbis Archives
The City of Manhattan Beach staff
Manhattan Beach Police Department
Community Police Academy
Blow by Bruce Porter
Law Enforcement in Manhattan Beach by Wm. R. Seidel
Easy Reader
Manhattan Beach News
The Beach Reporter
The Daily Breeze
100th Anniversary of Compton Centennial by Wanda McGreggor Allen
Fire Crackers—1944
Manhattan Beach Yesterdays

Jan Dennis
Researcher and Writer of
Manhattan Beach History

Introduction

In 1881, several years prior to the incorporation of what is now Manhattan Beach, the nation was reading about the shootout at the O.K. Corral in Tombstone, Arizona, and in 1901, when the first survey map of the Manhattan Beach township was filed, Butch Cassidy and his gang were holding up steam trains and robbing banks, with law enforcement in hot pursuit.

There were various titles for the guardians of the peace: town marshal, county sheriff, state or territorial ranger, federal marshal. A quote by the famous Sheriff Bat Masterson described these men very simply as "just ordinary men who could shoot straight and had the most utter courage and perfect nerve and for the most part, a keen sense of right and wrong".

In the late 1800s, unlike many of the other towns in Southern California which were settled and thriving, there was little need for law enforcement in the yet undeveloped area eventually destined to become the city of Manhattan Beach. The terrain along the ocean coastline was one of shifting sand dunes covered with scrub brush and flowers inhabited by small wildlife. By the early 1900s the human population began to grow along with township subdivisions. This would lead to residents petitioning the county for an independent municipality.

On December 2, 1912, with returns counted by the County Board of Supervisors, it was agreed that the territory was a duly incorporated municipal corporation of the sixth class, under the name and style of "City of Manhattan Beach," becoming a self-governing community with an elected Board of Trustees. On December 7, 1912, Secretary of State Frank C. Jordan endorsed the findings.

The newly incorporated town, with a population of approximately 600, many of whom were summer residents, was quick to put in place its own lawman. To present-day knowledge there were no shootouts in early Manhattan Beach. On December 21, 1912, at the second meeting of the Board of Trustees, the first peace officer, Fred W. Petway, was appointed City Marshal as well as first fire-fighting enforcement officer. He was on call 24 hours a day, 7 days a week, with little equipment or training for the apprehension of lawbreakers. In 1924, the city replaced the city marshal position with a chief of police. The police department as it is known today had marginal beginnings with little equipment or personnel training.

Many years would pass before a first class Police Department would oversee the safety and security of this growing community. During the city's 90 years of incorporation, there have been 3 Marshals and 11 Police Chiefs. The citizens of Manhattan Beach have always been extremely concerned with matters of public safety.

As the population increased so did the law enforcement organization, developing into an efficient, well-equipped, state-of-the-art agency. By 2003 the city's population was 34,514, and its police department, having a budget of $13,148,221 (38 percent of the City budget), had an authorized strength of 100 personnel which included 61 sworn officers. A dramatically different law organization exists today from that of the first security and safety operation.

Through photographs and text, this volume documents the development and historical events of a Police Department coming of age in a small family town on the shores of the Pacific Ocean. It cannot be overstated the many times a peace officer is put in harm's way or the spotlight that must be endured in handling high profile cases. These pages will take the reader through decades of men and women that have dealt with the risks, plans and frustrations in order to achieve the high standards of the Manhattan Beach Police Department existent today.

Marshals
Fred W. Petway 1912–1915
Fred W. Young 1915–1921
Bob "Dad" Kuhn 1921–1924

Chiefs
Fred J. Garvin 1924–1929
Harry S. Boardman 1929–1930
Alex Haddock 1930–1934
E. A. West 1934–1935
Henry G. Sights 1935–1956
Jerome "Jerry" Withers 1956–1969
Charles H. Crumly 1969–1971
Interim Co-Chiefs: H. Kuhlmeyer & H. O'Brien 1971–1974
Hugh H. O'Brien 1974–1980
Harry L. Kuhlmeyer 1980–1985
Ted Mertens 1985–1999
Ernest Klevesahl 1999–

Fishing off Manhattan Beach Pier was great! In the early days no one bothered to take his fishing pole and tackle home, as it was perfectly safe under the watchful eye of the local law enforcement.

One

Early Law Enforcement

In 1912 the City of Manhattan Beach was incorporated. Here, standing in front of the first city hall is Albert Clinton Conner, the newly elected city treasurer. The first building to serve as the city hall was originally the office of developer John Merrill, who did the intial survey map of the Manhattan Beach town site. The building was located in the 200 block of Center Street, now Manhattan Beach Boulevard.

Life prior to the city's incorporation was relatively simple; there was no need for a permanent law enforcement officer. There were few year-round residents and of those who did come to the beach came for sport fishing, clamming, and the enjoyment of the tranquil seaside. As for law and order in the new town, Frank C. Hill was selected City Attorney and the first peace officer; Fred W. Petway was appointed marshal. The first law enforcement case occurred in February 1913; a disturbance of the peace was charged against Joseph E. Hastings. Citizen Hastings had been arrested by Marshal Petway and found guilty and fined $15.00 by Judge C.E. Jenkins.

Marshal Fred W. Petway served the community from 1912 to 1915. He was required to be available 24 hours a day, seven days a week. The city paid so poorly for the position that Marshal Petway was obliged to work odd jobs to supplement his wage.

Little is known about the early criminal element in the new town. Nevertheless, there is one story that has been documented by many early settlers. When notified of an intruder at the Daugherty home, the marshal called for help in order to arrest the prowler. Since there was no jail facility in Manhattan Beach, a wagon was used to transport the prisoner to adjacent Hermosa Beach. During the trip the prisoner jumped from the wagon and started to run. Petway ordered the prisoner to halt. As the man continued to run, Petway discharged his shotgun and hit the prisoner in the leg. Instead of jail the man was taken to the hospital in Redondo Beach, further south. After learning he did not have the authority to use the weapon, Marshal Petway was so upset that he promptly resigned his position.

It was difficult for the Marshal to get around town before the streets were graded. After grades and elevations were determined, horses and mules were used to level the sand for paving, making it easier to maneuver around by foot, horse, or wagon.

This photo was taken of city hall at 15th Street and Highland Avenue shortly after its completion in 1917. The building also housed the police and fire departments.

The second City Marshal was Fred Young, serving from 1915 to 1921. In 1915 Young made George Whaton, J.H. Meadows, and L.H. Hatch deputy marshals. With the completion of the new city hall in 1916, one room and a jail cell for prisoners were made available on the second floor for the marshal's use. Police calls were received and relayed to the officer on duty by the firemen who worked 24-hour shifts. When an arrest was made at night the officer would awaken the fireman on duty and wait until he dressed and came upstairs to book the prisoner.

In late February 1917, while sawing wood at his home at 13th Street and Highview Avenue, Young glanced toward the newly completed city hall and saw smoke. Rushing into the house he told his wife to call the water department so that the water pressure would be maintained and then called for the Hermosa and Redondo Beach Fire Departments. A gale force wind was blowing, sucking the heat from the gas stove up the vent, making it red hot and causing the ventilator to ignite. The fire spread to the attic with flames shooting through the roof. Luckily, with the help of the Hermosa Beach Fire Department, the building was saved with a minimal amount of damage.

The Kuhn family found the community of Manhattan Beach to be very rural, with little relationship to the rapidly growing city of Los Angeles.

By 1921 Bob "Dad" Kuhn held the positions of water and street superintendent and building, gas and lighting inspector, in addition to the job of city marshal. In 1905, Kuhn, who was then a motorman on the Red Car trolley, had settled his family in Manhattan Beach. His term as marshal ran from 1921 to 1924. It was not unusual for the Marshal to have other employment, but after some residents complained about his cumulative salary, he resigned from his job as water and street superintendent in 1925.

One of the early problems the marshal encountered was the trafficking of illegal liquor. Prohibition was in effect, fostering the age of bathtub gin and bootlegging. The marshal, accompanied by others, staged raids at various locations within the city limits, netting not only contraband but also large sums of money. There were major establishments near the General Chemical Company as well as other parts of town where bootleggers worked out of their homes. During prohibition many men were taken into custody with bail set at $1,000. While Kuhn was marshal, there were many residents who felt the town was a virtual shooting gallery and the streets an auto racing track. The automobile industry had produced nearly two million new vehicles in 1920 and America was rushing into the auto age pell-mell. This seaside community was no exception. There was some kind of traffic encounter occurring almost weekly. Crime, too, was on the increase due to the availability of the car.

In 1921, hunting inside the town limits became a big headache for Marshal Kuhn. The city had enacted an ordinance prohibiting the shooting or discharging of any type of firearm, but the practice was still taking place. While in flight, sea birds were being shot for pure sport and the dead carcasses were washing up on the beach and left to decay. Signs were posted and it was the Marshal's job to curb the violations. Residents were encouraged to call when observing the practice.

While Kuhn was Marshal, there were many residents who felt that the town was virtually a shooting gallery and the streets were turning into auto racing tracks. In May of 1923, traffic officer Fred Garvin became the proud owner of a Henderson motorcycle. Its superior engineering firmly convinced him he now could keep up with the speeders.

The aerial view shows the pier area in the early 1920s. This locale was but a part of the vast

expanse that Marshal Kuhn and his volunteers had to cover.

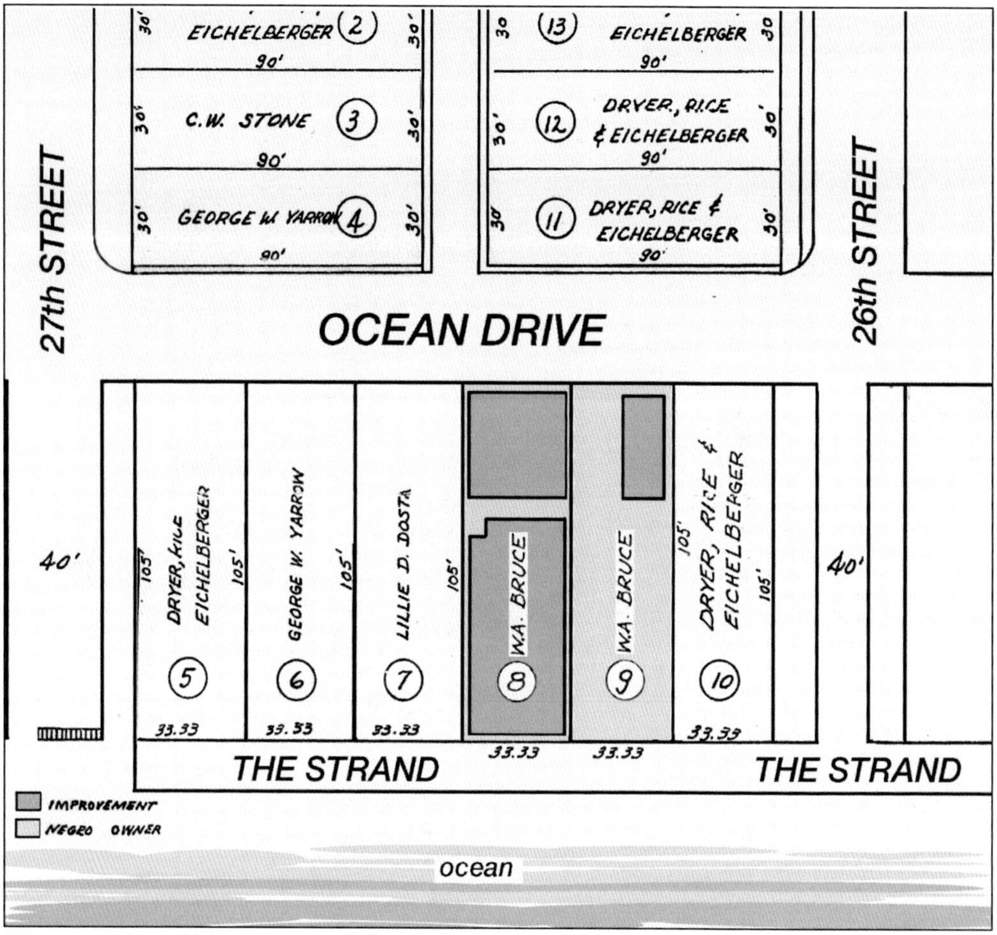

The map above depicts the ocean front area between 27th and 26th Streets in proposed condemnation proceedings for a public park. The shaded site, known as Bruce's Bathhouse, and other black-owned properties extended two blocks eastward.

In the mid 1920s while still dealing with the development of the town's infrastructure, Manhattan Beach residents were wrestling with controversial concerns. As in the rest of America, there was racial tension. The Ku Klux Klan was active around the country.

Throughout California their intolerance of minorities was strongly voiced and Manhattan Beach was not exempt from their doctrine of hate. Here in town they preached their message of racial prejudice under the name of "The White Legion."

Blacks had been coming to this area long before the town became a town. Many owned land between 26th and 27th Street adjacent to sand and surf. As the city grew, the response of the white community varied. The first "solution to the problem" was, in the mode of the times, segregation. The beach in front of Bruce's Bathhouse was fenced or roped off. However, blacks were still harassed and anyone who ventured beyond the boundary was arrested by the police and incarcerated. Having failed to drive blacks from Manhattan Beach, more drastic harassment ensued, resulting in the city imposing Ordinance #263 (February 7, 1924), condemning and acquiring all land west of Highland Avenue to the Strand between 26th and 27th street for the purpose of a public park. Although the ordinance was repealed on August 15, 1924, the legal battle went on for over four and a half years with the black families ultimately settling for favorable sale prices.

Two

A New Approach

In 1924, Manhattan Beach, with a population of 859, replaced its marshal program by creating a police chief position. Fred J. Garvin, who was the only motorcycle officer, became the city's first police chief (1924–1929). His department consisted of one other officer, Patrolman H.S. Boardman. The Chief traded 12-hour shifts with the patrolman; both worked seven days a week. They had to buy their own cars, uniforms, and weapons; the city did pay for the red lights and siren for the patrolman's car and furnished gas for the vehicles. There were no specific qualification requirements for employment, nor were the new policemen given any instructions.

The police department was formally organized in 1925 with 25 arrests made that year. In order to summon an officer, the city clerk, who was also desk sergeant, jailer, and judge, would turn on a red light that hung out of his office window.

"Sun, Sand, Sea, and Sky" was the attraction that brought celebrities and the general public to Manhattan Beach. During the depression decade, beach lovers could claim that, in the words of a popular song, "the best things in life are free." Any member of the City Council could tell you otherwise. The beach was a continuing expense for the city. One of the biggest expenses was due to the number of automobiles and visitors that multiplied the problems for the police. City officials complained that most people who used the beach lived elsewhere and therefore escaped paying taxes for beach maintenance.

With summer crowds, the department had to be expanded. Chief Garvin retired his position in 1929 and his only patrolman, Harry S. Boardman (1929–1930), became the new police chief. Parking problems and crowd control necessitated the hiring of more parking patrol officers. It was at this time that the city council employed two new patrolmen.

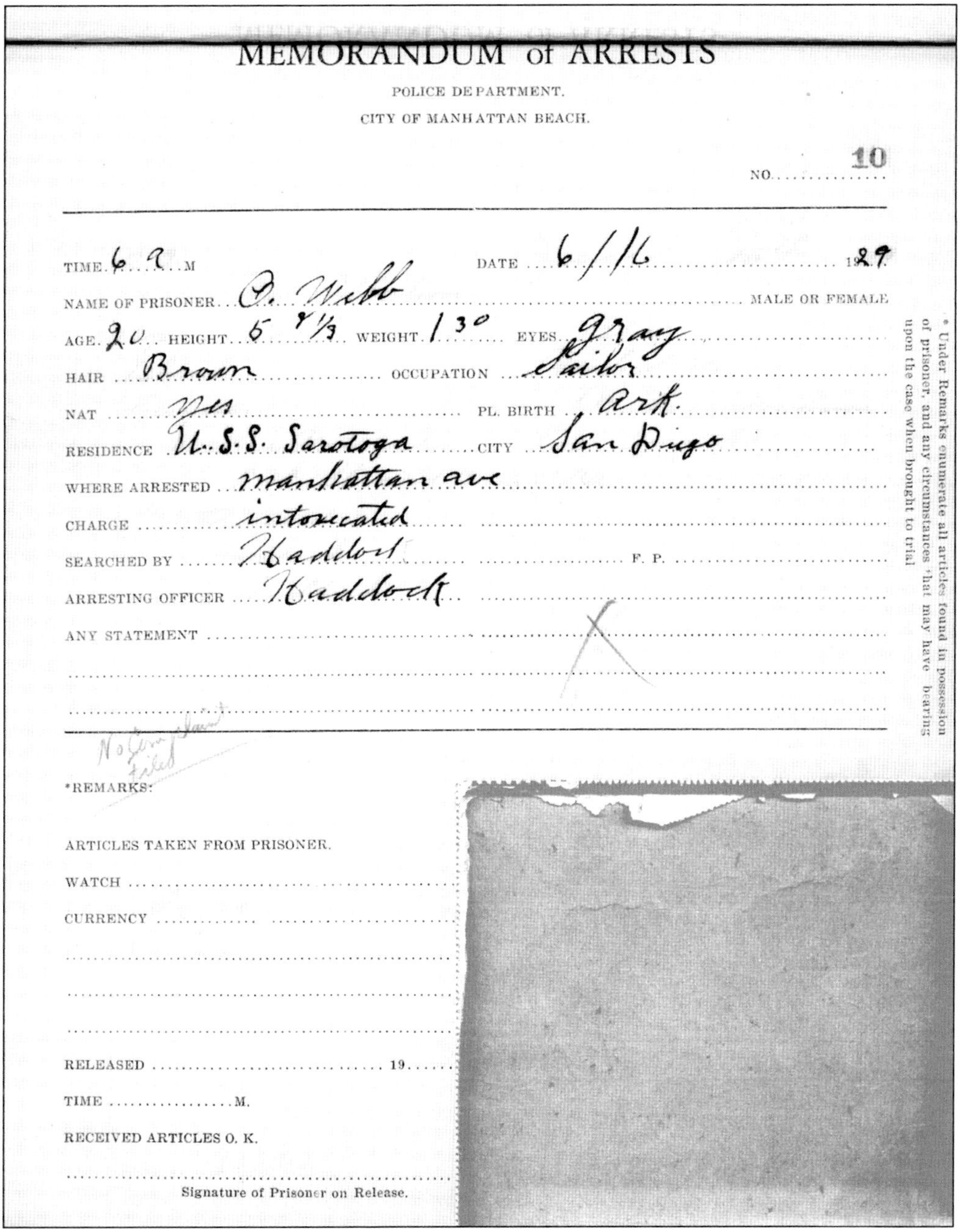

MEMORANDUM of ARRESTS

POLICE DEPARTMENT.

CITY OF MANHATTAN BEACH.

NO. 10

TIME 6 P. M DATE 6/16 1929

NAME OF PRISONER O. Webb MALE OR FEMALE

AGE 20 HEIGHT 5 8 1/3 WEIGHT 130 EYES Gray

HAIR Brown OCCUPATION Sailor

NAT yes PL. BIRTH Ark.

RESIDENCE U. S. S. Saratoga CITY San Diego

WHERE ARRESTED Manhattan ave

CHARGE intoxicated

SEARCHED BY Haddock F. P.

ARRESTING OFFICER Haddock

ANY STATEMENT

No Complaint filed

*REMARKS:

ARTICLES TAKEN FROM PRISONER.

WATCH

CURRENCY

RELEASED 19

TIME M.

RECEIVED ARTICLES O. K.

Signature of Prisoner on Release.

* Under Remarks enumerate all articles found in possession of prisoner, and any circumstances that may have bearing upon the case when brought to trial

Report writing was much simpler in 1929, as this exhibit from the first Memorandum of Arrests book indicates. A young sailor from the *U.S.S. Saratoga* stationed in San Diego was arrested for intoxication. The arresting officer was Alex Haddock, who would later become police chief.

In the spring of 1930, police officers found a 300-gallon illegal still in a house at 340 9th Street, a block east of the community church located on Highland Avenue. It had been installed in a bedroom, and a large storage tank was placed in the bathroom. Gas connections had been made with the main line, bypassing the meter, and a copper tube leading to a large galvanized tank at the side of the garage extending 30 feet south of the house. Chief Boardman kept a close surveillance of the property, arousing the operators' concern. When they did not appear at the house, the still was dismantled and taken to the station to await orders from the Federal authorities.

The illegal making of alcohol was not the only problem for Chief Boardman. Traffic at the beach was a "nightmare." Thousands of people came to the beach and onto the pier trying to catch that "big one". Nothing much mattered, not even the Great Bull Market crash of 1929. Parking problems and crowd control necessitated the hiring of more parking patrol officers. It all became too much for the Chief Boardman, who resigned in the latter part of June 1930, leaving five officers on the force, including two plain-clothes officers.

Alex Haddock, the third police chief (1930–1934), had been a member of the police department for four years, becoming police chief in the summer of 1930. Two of the biggest problems for Chief Haddock were the vast numbers of out-of-town visitors celebrating the beach seasons, and the smugglers bootlegging liquor. In order to have better contact with his patrolmen, three telephones were installed on poles around town so officers could check in with the desk.

The City Council hired three firemen to work 8-hour shifts on the police desk. Their duties were to answer both police and fire calls, and to book and care for prisoners. If the desk sergeant needed a patrolman he would turn on a red light, which had been placed on top of a pole that rose approximately 100 feet over the city hall. He then gave a few blasts of the air horn (installed in 1929). Rothwell Hunter Swain was one of the first desk sergeant firemen. In 1934 it was Swain who, after taking a course in fingerprint techniques through a mail-order correspondence school, would establish the records, fingerprint, and photographic departments.

In 1931, radio was used to promote Manhattan Beach over station KHJ and KFWB. The programming featured a discussion of the beautiful homes being built in town, real estate activity, and sundry matters of interest to prospective residents. However, there were others who found the isolated community ideal for clandestine reasons.

It was one of Chief Haddock's officers, Henry Sights, who observed barrels of liquor floating in the surf from a boat anchored off shore in El Porto (Manhattan Beach's north end). As the barrels came ashore the smugglers loaded the cargo into a van. Sights knew he could not take on the smugglers by himself and called the Hermosa Beach Police Department to stop the van. Federal agents were called in and seized the vehicle, placing it in the Hermosa Beach firehouse for safekeeping. The Manhattan Beach department was quite annoyed upon learning the "Feds" had acted without first notifying them. When it was time to move the van with its $30,000 cargo from the station, it became necessary to remove its wheels. It seems that many barrels had mysteriously disappeared. With the lightened load the suspension system of the vehicle was allowed to rise making it impossible to exit the doors without the drastic alteration.

Bootleggers would remain active until the 18th Amendment was repealed on June 27, 1933, abolishing prohibition. By July 13th, beer licenses were applied for and granted, however, only 3.2% alcohol beer could be served.

Beach-goers were still wearing the traditional full wool bathing apparel in 1931 when Hermosa Beach reformed their bathing suit ordinance by allowing children under the age of twelve to wear just trunks. However, Police Chief Haddock of Manhattan Beach was continuing to arrest bathers for wearing their swim attire in "any other manner than conventionally."

The Manhattan Beach dress Ordinance #368 was modified in 1933. Men were now allowed to sport bathing trunks on the beach and women could now wear two-piece suits. However, everyone had to "cover up" if walking on the pier or the Strand. This *Manhattan Beach News* cartoon depicts the attitude of the new bathing suit ordinance.

Pictured in 1934, from left to right, are: C. Whitehead, R.H. Swain, H.G. Sights, J. Root, A. Haddock, W. Ploter, and C. Koon. The new uniforms worn by the police force were navy blue, trimmed in gold stripes with brass buttons. During his tenure as police chief, Haddock held the position of president of the Fire and Police Association.

In 1934 the City Council exhibited firm control over the operations of the police department and Chief Haddock. Mayor Wedler charged him with "police laxity" for failing to kill a rabid dog quickly enough. The chief said that every effort had been made to investigate the case as reported to his officer and himself. They did not know the dog was rabid until after the animal had attacked two small children near the ocean.

Another issue Haddock faced was Wedler's opposition to the employment of an extra officer. Problems had been brewing for some time. While the Chief was on a business trip, the council fired a special duty police officer, Stanley Hall. Haddock had put Hall on the roster after consulting with the Police Commissioner as well as several of the Council members before making the appointment. It was explained that an added officer was needed due to recent thefts of plumbing fixtures and numerous other properties. The area to be patrolled was Blanche Road and Alma along with the municipal pier three nights a week. The mayor felt it was Haddock's responsibility to pay the officer's salary out of his own pocket.

Haddock was asked to resign because of insubordination. By mid-September of 1934, the mayor had succeeded in getting the council to demote Haddock back to officer status. The friction between the two men was not to last much longer. On November 1934, Haddock was dismissed from the police force upon charges presented by the mayor.

On September 28, 1934, the citizens of Manhattan Beach were introduced to their fourth police chief, E.A. West, who was a well-known lawman. West had joined the Los Angeles Police Department as a patrolman in 1912. For seven years he served as a traffic officer, plainclothesman, and detective. After resigning and going into business, he returned to police work in 1924, joining the Compton, California, Force. He became chief of Compton and served that post until 1932.

Unfortunately, in 1935, scarcely a year after arriving in Manhattan Beach, he resigned because of "political meddling." In that year there were 47 arrests made and 36 parking tickets issued.

Police files and records were practically nonexistent during this time. Officers acquired their education through the trial and error method, and by studying the Penal Code and the Vehicle Act.

While the police were having a bitter time with the city council and the mayor, the general population was having a wonderful time enjoying the sport of fishing.

Henry G. Sight, a native son of Pasadena, California, had been a resident of Manhattan Beach for 35 years before his appointment as chief of police. He had served the department since 1930 and became the fifth Chief on June 1935. He held that for 21 years. Like his predecessors, he had only two patrolmen, but started to reorganize the department by appointing six new patrolmen.

Under his watch, the first fingerprint card was filed in 1936 after taking the prints of Willie Wilson, a young black teenager. Other firsts followed; a darkroom was installed and the first bicycle license was issued. Two patrol cars were each outfitted with a First Aid kit, fire extinguisher, highway flares, and a radio receiving set tuned to Los Angeles' frequency, eliminating the red light on top of city hall.

A Junior Police Patrol was organized, consisting of 16 young boys of grammar school age. They were instructed in various elements of police work by the police officers that were trying to instill in the youngsters of the community the importance of staying away from criminally active youth gangs.

It was this home located on Second Street east of Sepulveda Boulevard that received international attention. Mystery and controversy confronted Chief Sights on September 26, 1936, when the body of Reid Russell was found shot to death in a garden swing on the estate that had been rented from a Mr. Morris.

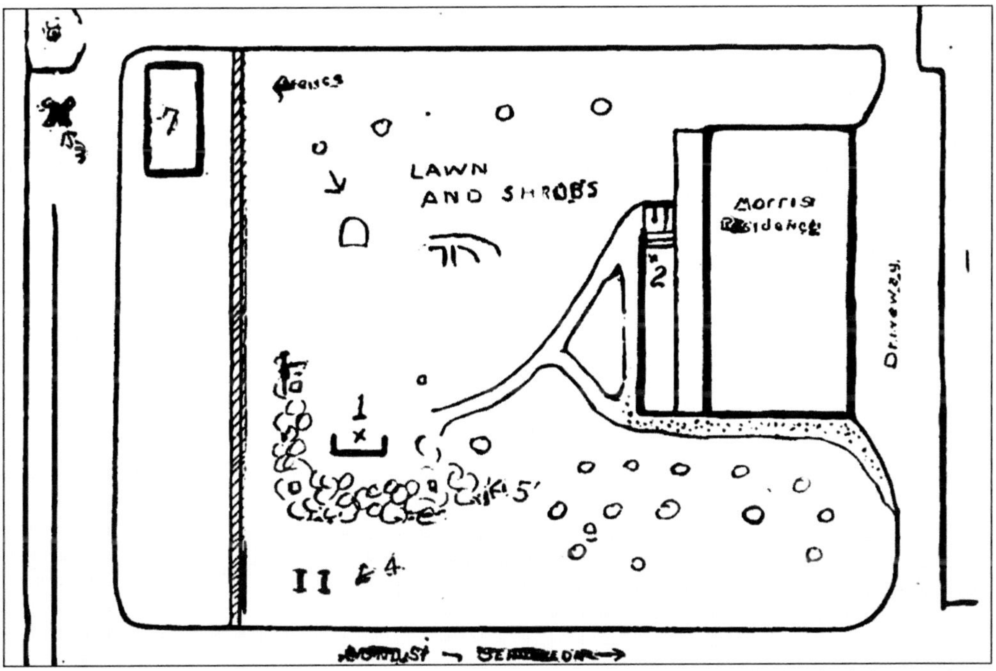

The diagram sketched by Sergeant Roth Swain indicates (1) location of the body, (2) area where Mrs. Morris and Lila Lee's young son, James Kirkwood Jr., was standing when they spotted the deceased. The body was lying on its back in the swing with a gun in its hand, but no cartridge casing was found. Even so, Police Chief Sights declared it a suicide and closed the case.

Left to right: Lila Lee, actress and former wife of actor James Kirkwood; Gouveneur Morris, a mystery novelist; Mrs. Morris; and Captain Clyde Plummer, chief of the District Attorney's Bureau of Investigation.

James Kirkwood Jr., while living with his mother and the Morris family in Manhattan Beach, attended Redondo Beach High School. He went on to become an actor and playwright, winning awards for cowriting "A Chorus Line" and credit for "Some Kind of Hero." His 1960 book, *There Must be a Pony*, portrayed the events surrounding the death of Reid Russell.

The re-enactment at the swing location left Captain Plummer and investigator Everett Davis with more questions that could not be answered. There were many contradictions in the case; for example, the Morrises told detectives that Reid had often talked of suicide and that a note was given to Mrs. Morris. When asked for the note she said she had burned it when she thought the case was closed.

Captain Plummer reopened the case at the request of Russell's mother, who did not believe her son would kill himself. Plummer believed the death to be a love-slaying, but there was another theory. It was felt that Russell might have met his death because he knew too much about an international smuggling ring. For several weeks the newspapers across the country printed various theories, and the case was reopened at least twice more, but no new evidence was found to determine how Russell died. To this day it remains an open case.

There were many more personalities living in Manhattan Beach during the '20s and '30s which brought the community and Chief Sights into the international spotlight. William Haines (right) was a matinee idol in the '20s at Metro-Goldwyn-Mayer. Jimmy Shields (left) was Haines' screen stand-in. Having been fired from MGM, Haines and Shields resumed their second careers, interior decorating, working for and with many of the Hollywood's famous personalities. Surrounded by many of their friends, Bill Haines and Jimmy Shields spent summers in a rented home on Moonstone Street located in El Porto (later annexed to the north end of Manhattan Beach).

The White League, Southern California's version of the Ku Klux Klan, also settled on the sunny shores of El Porto where they soon adorned their white robes to victimize residents of the community.

It was the third day of June in 1936 and a day of partying with friends on the sunny beach, where a local six-year old boy chased and played with a toy poodle belonging to Bill Haines. In the late afternoon on that fateful day the small boy, Jimmy Walker, was given 6 cents as a bribe to go home. It was this action, the parents' suspicion, and the fact the two men had been targeted for their lifestyle by the Klan that lead to a most regrettable scene. As the dinner guests were leaving the Haines' home, a white-hooded mob appeared warning them not to come back to the area. Shields and Haines were knocked to the ground, receiving black eyes and bleeding noses. Their cars were splattered with tomatoes and eggs, and the kicking of the dog left the poodle with serious injures.

After the attack, the remaining guests, Haines, and Shields were pushed into their car, never to return again. Normally the Manhattan Beach police would have come to the aid of the guests and residents, but without explanation they did not in this case.

Haines went on to become a world-renowned interior decorator. Yet so shaken by the horror of the experience it would be William Haines who would introduce the decorating world to colored bed linens. He was never again to adorn a bed with white sheets.

This photo captures little Jimmy Walker, his mother, and attorney on their way to court. The molestation case made world news but was dismissed due to a lack of evidence. However, the incident would always remain a very dark day in Manhattan Beach history.

In the period between 1936 and 1937 it was reported in the local newspaper, *Manhattan Beach News*, that there had been 4,791 police calls, 2,048 arrests, 923 traffic violations, and 142 drunk drivers. Child movie star Jackie Coogan was one of those given a citation for traveling on a Manhattan Beach street going 60 miles an hour in a 45 mile an hour zone. After missing two court appearances in Manhattan Beach City Hall, he pleaded guilty and paid a $15.00 fine.

Celebrities from the movie industry were always attracted to the unincorporated area called El Porto. Even its law enforcement officers were former cinema stars. Tom O'Brien, who starred in the classic film the *Big Parade*, and his partner Al Wolf, a master of ragtime piano, were assigned by the Sheriff's Department. Manhattan Beach Police were often called into the area even though El Porto was under the jurisdiction of the Los Angeles Sheriff's Department.

In 1937, "Jerry" Withers, a native son of Manhattan Beach, joined the department at the age of 27 as a patrolman. When he joined the force he was one of seven officers serving the city at that time.

This is the I.D. card issued to Jerry Withers when he joined the department. Interestingly, the photograph, which appears on the card, is not that of Withers but of Chief Sights.

The Police Department is photographed here in 1937: Jerry Withers appears third from the left and Chief Henry Sights stands next to the Department's matron at the right.

March 7, 1939, witnessed one of the most sensational stolen car captures in Withers' career. After a 95-mile-an-hour chase and three shots fired into the fleeing car, two male juveniles and a girl were placed in the Manhattan Beach jail. Withers is seen checking the car after the crash. A bullet hole can be seen in the center of the photo.

Chief Sights reported that the chase began when two of his officers, Jerry Withers and Ray Etienne, while making their usual evening rounds in the prowl car, observed a car that had been reported stolen. Jack Daro, Olympic Auditorium wrestling promoter, owned it.

The chase ended after the car skidded 217 feet before hitting a pole, shearing it off, and sliding an additional 38 feet before hitting another pole. The vehicle then bounced 30 additional feet before coming to a complete halt. Two of the three occupants received only scratches and bruises; however the second boy was badly injured.

In 1938 the State of California presented seven cities with safety awards. On May 13 of that year, a group of proud city officials accepted the "Honor City Plaque" from Ray Ingels, Director of Motor Vehicles. This photo was taken at the corner of 1st Street and Manhattan Beach Avenue, one of two locations where the city posted the award notices.

The Police Department officers and matron pose on the steps of City Hall for their 1939 Christmas postcard.

Three

A New Beginning

In 1937 the Works Progress Administration (WPA) constructed a 17-foot addition to the north side of city hall at a cost of $45,000. The department was now on the lower floor, with jail facilities and garage space for both police and fire apparatus. The north side of the city hall was cleared of 1000 square yards of sand and a large parking area was paved. The 1930s, with all its intrigue and bickering between the Police Department and city hall, were put to rest, at least for a short time.

In 1942, during World War II, the community saw not only officers going off to war, but also changes in the Police and Fire Departments. The two services were now separated; no longer did the fireman work the communications desk or book the criminals, nor did police personnel drive a fire truck. Now the police officers had to handle all of their own duties. This created a burden for Chief Sights, who now had to pull patrolmen out of the field to work the desk. To make matters worse, the postwar population was exploding. The eleven officers were working around the clock.

Jerome "Jerry" Withers had been an officer for nine years when he joined the Coast Guard in September 1942. After serving 18 months as chief gunner's mate in the North Pacific aboard the frigate USS Albuquerque, he returned to the police force in 1944.

During the war years, instructions were posted for city residents and workers detailing procedures to be taken in the event of an air-raid attack. It was quite clear no employee was to stop work unless intructed to do so. Camouflage netting used on many public and business buildings served to heighten the awareness of the war effort at home.

When the Police Department was separated from the Fire Department, not only did the police uniforms change to dark blue, but the badge was replaced by a star, which took on a different graphic design.

The new badge.

MANHATTAN BEACH POLICE DEPARTMENT

Driver____________________ Date____________194__

The Police Officer has been obliged to caution you because of an infraction of the law. Remember, careless driving jeopardizes the lives of others, as well as that of yourself.

Every time you start your car in operation, remember "JACKIE".

Please be careful! We want to enlist you as one to aid us in promoting safety ALWAYS.

Sincerely yours,
HENRY G. SIGHTS
Chief of Police

____
Police Officer

(See Over) **VIOLATION**

Jackie

(The Son of a Hard-boiled Cop)

You think I'm a hard-boiled copper
Writing tickets at forty-three
Well, perhaps I'm thinking of Jackie,
And all that the lad meant to me.

How's that? Tell you about it?
Well, stranger, the boy was my son.
God what I'd give to hear "DADDY"
Once more when the day's work is done.

The driver was just in a hurry;
He didn't intend any harm,
But the sun and the stars quit shining
When I picked up my boy's lifeless form.

Well, Mister, I'll not give you a ticket;
I don't want to "pinch" any one..
But I'd ride this motorcycle through hell
To protect another man's son.

So the next time you feel like speeding
Or passing a boulevard STOP,
Just pause and Remember my Jackie,
The son of a hard-boiled cop.

(See Over)

Chief Sights understood the need for education and required officers to attend all available schools offering instruction in law enforcement, procedures, and methods. In 1944 there were approximately 4,216 criminal record cards on file in fingerprint classification. In that same year there were 1,400 arrests, many of them traffic infractions. To bring the point of safe driving to the public's attention, he devised the "violation card." This card, with its warning on the front and the poignant poem on the reverse side, was handed out to violators of every observable traffic offense.

As the world's largest flying boat, Howard Hughes' experimental airplane the "Spruce Goose", moved through the South Bay on its way to Long Beach; it was a Manhattan Beach motorcycle officer who escorted the craft along Sepulveda Boulevard. Shown here is the left wing of this gigantic plane as it went up the hill.

In November of 1948, at the corner of 30th and Sepulveda Boulevard, a driver failed to observe oncoming traffic. He may have stopped as required, but failed to yield to oncoming traffic, creating an immediate hazard. This accident was used as an example to reinforce the department's message, "Remember, careless driving jeopardizes the lives of others."

By the end of the 1940s the police force had three patrol cars and two motorcycle officers (referred to by the Department as Motor Officers). Officer Bob Carstens, who stood 6 foot 4 inches, appears on the far left.

In 1949, Officer Brent Grey is displaying his uniform and motor. It was shortly after this photo was taken that officers were required to wear hard helmets.

Three-way radios were installed in April 1940 and assigned to the City of El Segundo frequency. During this time the department broadcast calls for neighboring Redondo and Hermosa Beach, where they were transferred to Manhattan's wavelength, thereby maintaining close contact with four South Bay communities.

Drivers of autos and motors could now talk to the home station. That same year, 1950, a Teletype machine was installed in the department, facilitating the reception of information for reception and transmission anywhere in Los Angeles County.

The city was steadily growing in 1953; there was a population of 26,315, 96.5 miles of street to patrol, and a city tax rate of $1.73. And so grew the police force. Chief "Hank" Sights and

Assistant Chief "Jerry" Withers (center) were in charge in 1955.

On December 16, 1955, Chief Sights, who had joined the Department in 1929, was amongst those receiving a diamond-studded pin signifying a minimum of 25 years of service. Joining him are, left to right: Clarence Koon, who entered the police department in 1927; Leonard Olson of the water department, who started in 1930; and Fire Chief Rothwell Swain, who also began his career with the city in 1929.

The Police Department contained some of the finest marksmen. In 1938 the pistol range was built just southwest of Blanche Road and Rosecrans. This range was considered the finest in California. Credit for its excellent construction work went almost entirely to the personal efforts of the local police officers, who devoted their off-duty hours to digging post holes, grading, erecting fences, and building the range house.

After 21 years of service, Chief Henry G. Sights retired. His assistant, Jerome "Jerry" Withers was appointed the new Chief on November 29, 1956. The department also added a new lieutenant and captain, making a force of 30 officers receiving 7 paid holidays a year and a salary of $413 a month. For a town approximately 4 square miles, 128,738 miles were patrolled during that year. Statistics proved crime was on the increase with 876 arrests for misdemeanors, 105 for felonies, and 455 juvenile cases processed. But it was the political and internal issues that challenged Withers through the remainder of the 1950s.

In June of 1957, Withers fired Officer Chester G. Hansen for misconduct, incompetence, inefficiency, and failure to perform his duties as a policeman. However, after several weeks of hearings, Hansen was found not guilty of all charges. He later resigned and joined the San Fernando Police Department.

Due to public insistence, Chief Withers' department began a crackdown on sexual perversion, which was taking place on the beach and in public rest rooms. A two-month investigation by two undercover detectives was responsible for the arrest of 30 people on sexual charges resulting in a 100 percent conviction rate.

Here are a few officers on a summer day. The uniform regulations allowed officers to wear open collar sport-type shirts only between May 1st and September 30th. During the rest of the year, ties were to be worn at all times, except when detectives wore special clothing for stakeouts. Female personnel also abided by these regulations.

It was not all work for many of the officers; a softball team was formed in 1957. Appearing from left to right are: Chief Jerry Withers, Don Stone, John Morrow, Fred Arenz, unknown, Hugh O'Brian, Harry Kuhlmeyer, and Bob Heathcote.

Prior to 1958, the injuries to officers were not life-threatening, but because of faster motorcycles and automobiles speeding along the streets, several officers came very close to being killed. Motorcycle Officer Harold T. Britton, age 28, was chasing a speeding car when another vehicle pulled out from a side street and collided with Britton, throwing him from his motor. Fortunately he suffered only minor cuts and bruises and a torn uniform. A similar accident occurred to motorcycle officer Charles C. Knight, who sustained serious injuries.

Ground breaking for the new Police Station saw Assistant Police Chief Lelan A. Foster (left) with shovel in hand and Police Chief Jerry Withers (right) holding the second shovel (others not identified).

When completed in 1958 at a cost of $185,000, the new, furnished and modern 10,000-square-foot police facility relieved the overcrowded quarters in the city hall. The station had a separate locker-room for the officers, kitchen area in the squad room, jail for housing 26 prisoners, drunk tank, and the very finest equipment. Law enforcement personnel occupied the new quarters in 1959, confident that the department now had the ability to keep up with increased demands. Three women were hired to work the new communications desk. Each woman worked one 8-hour shift around the clock, 24 hours a day, 7 days a week. This released the police officer who had been working the desk to enter the field. The department had 30 officers who included 4 detectives and 4 motor officers. The department could field 7 patrol cars at this time.

Not so confident was the working atmosphere. Personnel, rather than the new environment, had become the topic of the day. In 1957 the Manhattan Beach Civic Association asked the District Attorney's Office to do an internal investigation of the police department. They charged that supervisors were harassing police officers and favoritism was being shown in the appointment of officers to higher rank. The Chief held the entire force incommunicado for 15 hours, during which time they were not allowed to call home and an investigation was conducted. In February of 1958, again the Chief Withers had an officer on the "Carpet," charged with misconduct, incompetence, inefficiency, and failure to perform polices duties and follow the department's rules and regulations. He was also charged with mistreatment of prisoners. Manley Lyle Fox was given a public Civil Service hearing and found guilty of the charges. Fox was no longer a member of the department.

Four

Big Time Crime

The decade of the 1960s began with residents of the city enjoying one of the lowest crime rates in the county. The police force was well acquainted with the town and its people, creating an easy-going relationship. However, the demands on law enforcement were about to change. Increasing criminal mobility, a larger population, and complex police procedures would alter law enforcement operations to a greater degree than any other city service.

By 1960, the civic center was complete with a new police complex and a new Fire Station. The next 20 years would see better trained and more involved officers. With the new facility came "Police Tools," which were greatly needed in the apprehension of law breakers and the safety of the community.

In 1960, there were 45 uniformed personnel in the department. From left to right are the Officers of the Traffic Enforcement: Ernie Schultz, Bob Carstens, Dave Cooper, Norman Hall, William Walker, unknown woman, Phil Walker, and Bill Pettit.

Training became a major recruitment qualification for all officers. No longer were they appointed by the city council, but they were required to take a Civil Service examination. New officers were now sent to the County Sheriff's Academy for 16 weeks. The salary for 80 of the first 160 hours of training was paid by the State; Manhattan Beach was the first city to qualify for the State Salary Reimbursement Plan. Officers were also selected for additional schooling at the F.B.I. Academy in Washington D.C., various universities and surrounding colleges. After the Academy, the trainee continued his education for six weeks to two months with the assistance of an officer at the station.

Chief Withers gave new officers a manual for guidance and direction while on duty. They had to become thoroughly familiar with the rules and regulations set forth in the manual.

Officer Bob Carstens joined the force on June 1, 1948, and became an integral part of the department. Before the station had a place for the reloading of gun shells, Carstens did the work in his garage.

By 1962, an ammunition loading room was provided at the station.

This is one of the many pistol ranges available to Manhattan Beach officers.

Through the years, there have been several police pistol teams representing Manhattan Beach. These teams were skilled and proficient, scoring high honors while traveling to various locations. In 1962 and 1963 the pistol team participated in 24 matches, losing only 4. At that time the team was formed of Don Stone, Lieutenant Ernest Schultz, Dan Wagner, Robert Perry, and Gene Watts.

Many were the honors and trophies won by four of the Manhattan Beach Pistol Team.

In 1964 the sharp shooters of the day were, from left to right: Don Lastra,"Loredo Lud" Frank Lodwick, Ray Burgess, and "Slats Stone" Don Stone.

Motorcycle Officer Richard "Tim" Giles joined the force on December 1, 1958, and was the first Manhattan Beach police officer killed in the line of duty February 16, 1962.

While talking to an off-duty police officer, Officer Giles observed a car traveling at a high rate of speed. With siren on, he was in hot pursuit. The chase continued northward on Sepulveda Boulevard until a car pulled out into Giles' path.

At the corner of 6th Street and Sepulveda Boulevard, Giles and his motorcycle collided with the intruding car, causing Giles' body to be thrown several feet over the car. Officer Giles died of his injuries a few hours later.

On March 23, 1962, the community, along with the Police Department, put on a variety revue at Mira Costa High School Auditorium. The Memorial Benefit Show was a fundraiser for the education of Officer Giles' two sons, Donald, age 6, and Daniel, age 3.

Among the personalities attending the benefit was Hal Peary, honorary Mayor of Manhattan Beach and star of the popular radio show *The Great Gildersleeve*. He served as master of ceremonies. Singer Linda Lee is shown being interviewed by Mr. Peary. Other talents included well-known musical recording group the Beach Boys.

In 1963, while a work crew was grading Valley Drive between 15th Street and 10th Place, a young workman was trapped by a sand cave-in. Officer Bill Pettit is shown helping to place the injured man into an ambulance, while Lieutenant Ernest W. Schultz, (his back to the camera and wearing a plaid jacket) investigates the accident.

On occasion, traffic violations could take a unique turn. From left to right, Manhattan Beach Officers Fred McKewen and Reuben Santillanes were obliged to give a ticket to a Santa Fe Railroad train which had blocked Rosecrans Avenue for more than the five minutes allowed by the city ordinance. The obstruction of through traffic for more than 10 minutes caused a back up of over 100 cars.

In the 1960s, the Detective Bureau and Administration staff of the department saw an increase in homicides, robberies, and narcotics. The group was comprised of (from left to right) J.A. Smith, Gene Guitare, Ray Bennett, Frank Lodwick, John Morrow, Frank Jeffers, Chuck Cohen, Hugh O'Brien, and Chief Jerry Withers.

A traffic safety program was brought into the primary school classes by the Dolphins, a women's community organization. Shown above are children being introduced to Rueben Santallanes as "Officer Friendly."

On March 4, 1966, Betty Andrews and Jim Deneui took part in the 109th graduation exercises at the Police Academy in Los Angeles. Betty became the second policewoman to serve on the Manhattan Beach Police Force. From left to right are: Assistant Chief Justus Smith, Policewoman Betty Andrews, Officer Jim Deneui, and Sheriff Peter J. Pitchess.

Policewoman Betty Andrews worked side by side with department officers as they check the paper work for motorcycles and bicycles as a part of the safety program.

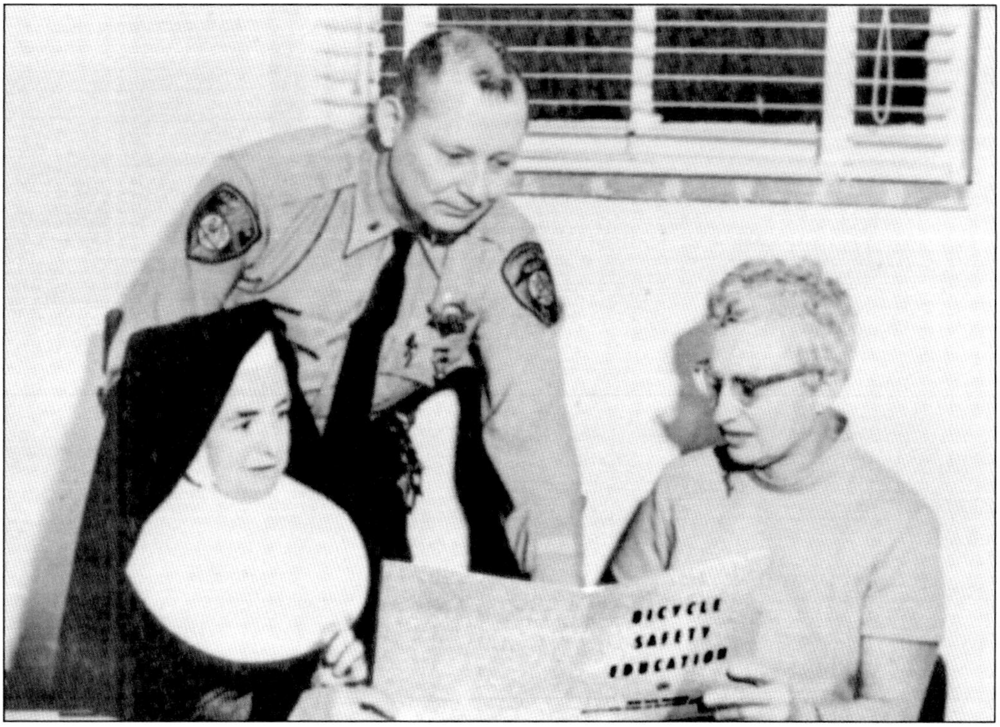

American Martyrs School was involved with the bicycle safety education program. Sister Ruth Ellen, principal of the school, Miss Gerling, Safety Chairman, and Lieutenant Bill Schultz evaluate the subject material, which was used for instructional purposes by all teachers participating in the program.

Police are working in one of the local schoolyards, checking bicycle license registration while reviewing basic traffic rules and instructions on safety.

A perplexed meter officer exemplifies the parking dilemma caused by an ever-increasing population of residents and summer visitors. In 1967, there were 30,377 parking citations issued, making it almost impossible for the police department to keep abreast of the acute parking problem. Part of that problem was the 400 percent annual escalation of motorcycles.

Aside from parking, the problem of general traffic expansion prompted the installation of special police cars with radar equipment in order to maintain better accident control at such busy intersections as Rosecrans Avenue and Sepulveda Blvd.

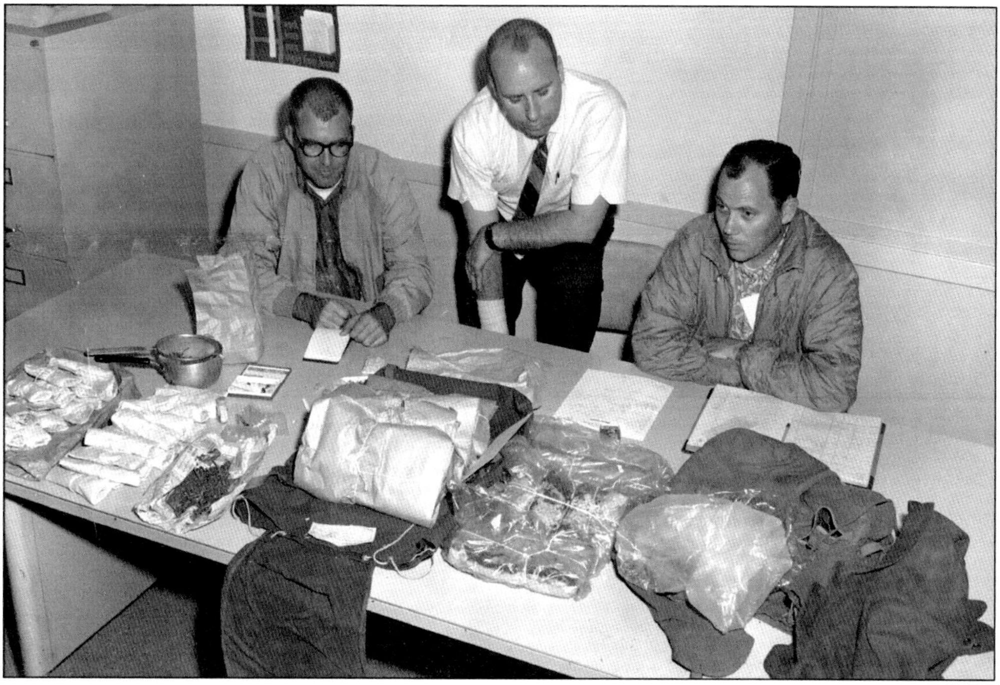

Crime was escalating. Narcotics and hallucinatory pills had become alarmingly prevalent. Law enforcement was doing all they could to make the community aware of the dangers of drug abuse. Shown above, Officers Fred McKewen at center and William Walker on the right side, (officer on left not known) display 15 kilos of marijuana seized in a raid, resulting in two arrests. Besides the drug problem, the department was faced with its first bank robbery in November 7, 1963.

After a drug raid, Lieutenant Williams Pettit, chief of the city's detective bureau, weighs narcotics that included a pound of opium. The raid, where $7,000 worth of drugs were seized, was carried out by Manhattan Beach police, El Segundo police, and the Federal Narcotics Bureau.

George Jung, fresh and clean-cut looking, graduated from high school in 1961 in Weymouth, Massachusetts. Later, at the age of 25, he came west to California and Manhattan Beach. On the surface, this seaside city in 1967 might have appeared to many as a quiet, low profile community. To others, however, it was labeled as the reigning party town on California's southern coast. There is little wonder that this young man of the '60s generation thought he had found paradise.

George wanted wealth, and in the temper of the times, what better way than to get into the drug trade. To George this was the place—close to the Los Angeles International Airport and close to the Mexican border. The Manhattan Beach Police Department had only one narcotics officer, 31-year-old Detective Fred McKewen, who had no budget for launching undercover operations. Being easily recognized by all the drug dealers in town made his job doubly difficult. While McKewen did work with U.S. Customs, as well as Federal and State agencies, he was never able to arrest Jung.

However, George was finally caught and sent to prison after a lifetime of using and selling drugs. He made approximately $100 million dollars before losing it all. George Jung's story and his involvement with the narcotics business can be read in the book *Blow*, written by Bruce Porter.

George Jung, blond, with hazel-green eyes and a hefty physique, is seen here in 1970 in Mazatlan doing business with one of his colleagues (name unknown).

Once again, on a return to the area of his younger days, George Jung is seen in 1991 on The Strand in Manhattan Beach.

It could have been right out of an old western novel. On March 1968, the corner of 8th Street and Sepulveda Boulevard became the site of the shoot-out at the El Rancho Motel. Thirty-five-year-old Arthur Glen Jones, who had escaped from San Quentin prison, had been serving a life term for murder. Barricaded in a motel room, he told police he would not be taken alive and refused to come out. Jones set off several sticks of dynamite in the room, causing some damage. After tear gas was fired into the room by Detective Don Stone who was first on the scene, Jones dove through the window firing his gun at the officers. A hail of police bullets followed. Officer Bill Smalley is caught on camera with his weapon trained on the fugitive, who lay on the ground dying.

Police reported that Jones had been convicted in San Bernardino in the 1959 killing of a Redlands tavern owner.

By 1969, Chief Withers decided to retire, and on September 3, 1969, Charles W. Crumly became the seventh Police Chief of Manhattan Beach. Crumly did not come from the rank and file of the department, but was a retired captain in the Los Angeles Police Force. To some Crumly was considered an "outsider."

With a new Chief came the introduction of the new all-white police cars, shown here with Officer Don Stone. The police department switched to all-white vehicles in an effort to "soften their image" and to boost the morale of the force.

Pictured are Chief Charles Crumly (middle center left), Assistant Chief Justus A. Smith (middle center right), and the other officers of the Department. In October 1969, Crumly reorganized the Police Officer Reserve program, which required all new candidates to be between 26 and 45 years of age, a minimum weight of 145 pounds, residents of the city, and willing to serve without pay. The department conducted the training and supplied the equipment. Trainees were to work a minimum of four eight-hour shifts a month.

Chief Crumly also reorganized the department to improve the utilization of manpower. Some felt that he was trying to reorganize too fast. It was a known fact that maintaining the safety of the community in an era of increasing crime was a day-to-day challenge for the force. During the early years, with a fragmented organization, the staff was not very efficient. It was not a cost-efficient operation either. One of the first things the new chief did was to create three divisions: patrol, investigation, and administration. A captain was put in charge of each division. Prior to this time the department operated with a four-position management staff: chief, assistant chief, and two captains.

In December of 1969, working to promote a positive image of the police department to the community, resident Jan Dennis asked the city to purchase a living tree to be decorated by school children in the community. Shown standing before the prominently placed tree in the city's popular Polliwog Park are, from left to right, Captain Hugh O'Brian, Jan Dennis, and Chief Crumly.

Keenly aware of the positive attention given to the department, Police Chief Crumly also accepted Dennis' additional idea of police involvement in the event by bringing Santa in a "black and white" with officers participating as helpers.

Officer Pete Beaman helps seven-year-old Jennifer Farris place her hand-made decoration on the community Christmas tree.

Chief Crumly was seriously concerned with the rise in crime. The department's achievement of a 2.47 percent reduction in major crimes over the previous year and a 39 percent increase in arrests reflected his focus on this problem in 1971.

With Chief Crumly on a leave of absence after suffering a heart attack, Captian Harry Kuhlmeyer and Captain Hugh O'Brien took over the Chief's duties. In 1972, O'Brien was appointed Acting Chief of Police of Manhattan Beach

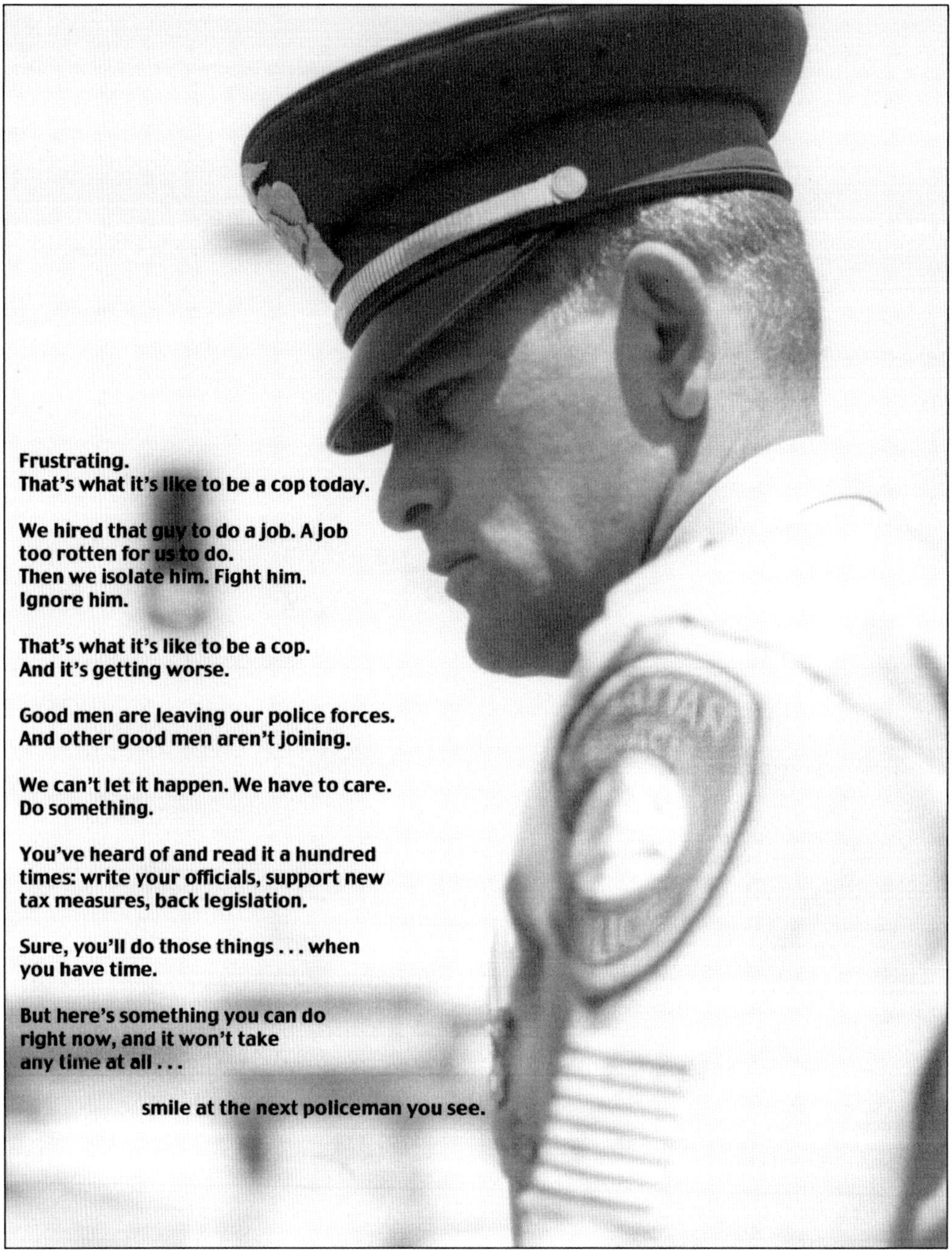

In the 1960s police departments around the country felt a lack of respect from much of the population. The author, to ease the frustration of the local police department, produced this flyer. Here, Officer Ray Schott represents the Manhattan Beach Force.

Five

COMMUNITY RELATIONS

The 60th Anniversary of the City's Incorporation was celebrated in December of 1972. A parade with the Police Color Guard led the way. The Guard was comprised, from left to right, of Officers Raymond Burgess, Daniel P. Kuhn, and David R. Goss.

Chief Crumly's reorganization of the police department brought the age of the computer to the station. In October of 1971, the Technical Services Division began training for on-line operations scheduled for January of 1972.

The population of the community continued to grow; in 1974 it was over 35,000 and capital improvements were the order of the day. At a cost of $250,000, a three-level parking structure consisting of 150 spaces was built at 12th Street and Morningside Drive and dedicated in late 1971. This facility brought more cars to the Central Business District, creating more problems for the traffic control officers.

On October 16 1972, Jane Hoag joined the Manhattan Beach Police Force. When classification was changed from policewoman to police officer, Jane became the first female Investigating Officer in 1987.

Pictured above is Lieutenant Kent Mastick. In 1974, the population was approximately 35,000 and the Police Department consisted of 53 policemen whose starting salary was $930 a month. These figures had changed considerably since 1951 when the population was 20,000 and 16 policemen received a monthly salary of $275. An officer still had to buy his uniform and weapon, but by 1975 the department provided each officer with safety equipment and a Smith & Wesson model 67 stainless steel revolver.

In 1972, Officer Robert Carstens retired from the department. His long and distinguished service had made him a legend. He had been referred to as a "cops' cop" and an "all around great officer."

For several years Santa came by way of a police car to visit the children at the Manhattan Heights Elementary School. Community involvement was becoming extremely important.

SPECIAL BULLETIN

Manhattan Beach Police Officers' Association, Inc.
P.O. Box 1542, Manhattan Beach, California 90266

PLEASE POST

FRIDAY • COCKTAILS - 6:30 P. M. (No Host Bar) DINNER - 7:30 P. M. • 6-14-74

TESTIMONIAL DINNER HONORING

28 YEARS POLICE SERVICE

ASSISTANT CHIEF JUSTUS A. SMITH

(TICKETS - $6.50 PER PERSON, INCLUDES TAX, TIP AND GIFT. CONTACT OFFICERS MC KEWEN, WEHNER OR BETTY WILLITS - 545-4566.)

LOCOCO'S 612 SEPULVEDA M.B.

WANTED

Assistant Chief Justus A. Smith joined the department in May of 1946; however, he left the force when he was called to active duty in the U.S. Air Force. He returned in 1955. There were many who felt Assistant Chief Smith should have been appointed Police Chief when Chief Crumly retired. Smith's retirement party on June 14, 1974 honored his 24 years and 8 months of service on the force.

In 1975 the front desk and the city's jail facilities were upgraded in order to meet state standards. For the first time there would be an in-house food preparation system for the jail.

Officer Don Stone relays to Santa his wish for the holiday at the Christmas party given by the police department for officers' children and families. Sitting at the right is Officer Frank Frazier.

Like the open houses at the station, schools were encouraged to bring their students for a tour of the facility. Here in 1974, a group of young children from one of the grade schools pose for their souvenir photo.

Following the retirement of Chief Crumly in 1974, Captain Hugh H. O'Brian was appointed Manhattan Beach's 8th Police Chief. He had been on the force since 1954, after serving with the El Segundo Police Department for two years. He rose through the ranks quickly with a wealth of "street smarts" and education. Like his predecessor, O'Brian was interested in community relations. He started a speaker's bureau, which provided officers the opportunity to speak at Parent-Teachers Associations and service clubs. He also created the ride-along program for the community, enabling them to become better acquainted with the officers and their law enforcement operations.

A quote from Sergeant Jack Zea in 1987 reflects the respect felt for him, "He had a real, true feeling for the officers who worked for him. He was able to make hard decisions but he considered the officers before he made the decisions".

Of course, there were some days when things just didn't go as planned!

On March 20, 1975, the first Awards Luncheon was held to honor individual police and firemen who had distinguished themselves by conspicuous bravery, courage, or outstanding meritorious action. It had been developed by a committee of the Joint South Bay Chambers of Commerce.

There were thirteen South Bay Officers who received medals and plaques at the first Awards Luncheon. Dimly seen in the photo are the Chiefs' badges of the South Bay city display behind the recipients.

Officer Steven Stone and Jim Noble were the first two Manhattan Beach Officers to receive the honor. Their heroism was noted when they pulled a man and woman from an automobile that was fully engulfed in flames, putting them in life-threatening danger. The woman survived; however, the male victim later died.

A closer camera view shows the two officers who received special recognition from State Attorney General Evelle Younger. Appearing from left to right are Officer Jim Noble, Mr. George Gessie, Officer Steve Stone, his mother Mrs. Stone, and father Officer Don Stone.

There were always large groups of both children and adults who attended the open house activities at the station.

The children get an opportunity to examine one of the motorcycles used by the traffic division and meet some of the officers.

On June 25, 1976, the entrance to the pier was closed by order of Police Chief O'Brian. The County lifeguards had requested the closure following a week of rioting by an estimated 1,000 young people. Many of the youths were jumping off the pier, an illegal practice that had plagued lifeguards for days, and resulted in the death of a boy. Officers were being pelted with rocks and sand-filled bottles. Support came with the arrival of more than 80 police officers, including sheriff's deputies and police from four cities.

The crowd was forced away from the pier and The Strand toward Manhattan Avenue. Several adults and juveniles were arrested by the time it was all over.

As the riot continued, separate incidents would erupt causing on-lookers to gather. The Police would arrive quickly to quell the fight and keep the order. The ages of the youths ranged from pre-teens to young adults.

January 5, 1977, introduced one of five new Chevy Nova black and white police patrol cars driven by Officer Bob Bey. The department switched from all white cars to black and white vehicles in an effort to make them more easily recognized by the public.

By 1977, department officers, on average, could claim having acquired 86.7 college units (equivalent to 2.9 years of higher education) in addition to 60 hours of in-service training a year. A sample of these well-qualified officers of the 1970s is, from left to right, Steve Hosepian, Mike Carra, Bill Bartz, and Bill Sapp. There was extensive emphasis on specialized training and education certified by the California Commission of Peace Officers Standards and Training (P.O.S.T.).

In 1978, Chief O'Brian (standing) and Officer Fred McKewen (right) congratulate Officer Art Langstaff upon receiving the Chamber of Commerce Rose and Scroll Award. Officer Langstaff at this time was an 18-year veteran of the Manhattan Beach Police Department.

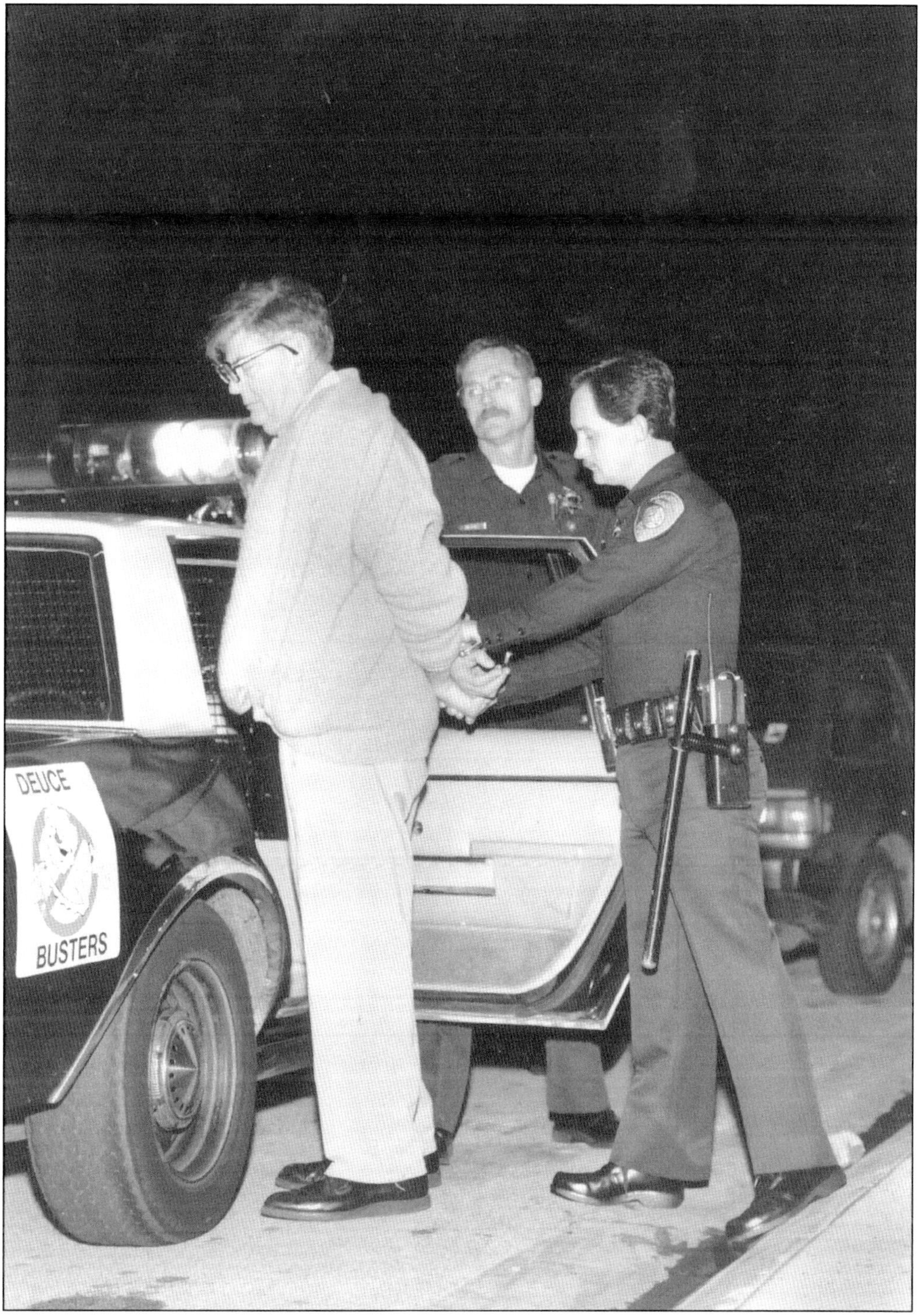

The action shown here is a routine training exercise in the proper method for subduing a driver under the influence of alcohol or drugs. Here Officer John Hensley handcuffs a "suspected drunk driver."

The city management proposed that the Police and Fire Departments be combined in order to save money. The concept of public safety involves the basic cross-training of all public safety personnel in law enforcement, fire fighting, and first aid. It entailed additional training for both the Police and Fire Departments. It was suggested that basic fire fighting training for police personnel could be accomplished with approximately 25 hours of instruction. Several communities had such an arrangement, but it was not well received by the Manhattan Beach Police Force. The picketing of City Hall by the men in blue was proof of that.

Officer Art Langstaff's placard said it all: "Big Savings But At What Cost?"

In 1979, Detective Vince Leone found more than vegetables growing in this resident's back yard. In an attempt to disguise the marijuana plants, red balls had been tied to their branches to imitate tomato vines.

Narcotics Detective Fred McKewen, with Officer John Wehner looking on, displays the marijuana plants after they were taken out of the ground and brought to the station.

Detectives Langstaff and McKewen cut up and box the marijuana plants which were then sent to the L.A. Sheriff's Department for destruction.

From 1973 to 1993, Mrs. Anita Spikula was the Detective Bureau's secretary and "den mother." There were six detective officers in the department handling robbery, narcotics and burglary, auto theft, check and bunco, and juvenile.

In 1980, a citizen's committee for the purpose of establishing and maintaining healthy and cooperative relations between the police and the citizens of the community developed the Neighborhood Watch Program. In the year 2003, four hundred block captains provide a communication link between the police and the residents in their respective blocks.

Harry L. Kuhlmeyer was appointed the 9th Manhattan Beach Police Chief on the 27th of September 1980. He had been with the department since 1953 and served as a captain for 16 years. Prior to joining the department he served as a police officer in the City of Santa Monica for six years. It was his plan to continue the use of the Neighborhood Watch Program and make more extensive use of the K-9 patrols as an effective crime prevention tool.

After nearly 30 years of wearing the traditional beige shirt and dark green pants, the old uniforms were shed to conform to most other police agencies. In June 1981 police personnel were now wearing blue uniforms that were paid for with the officers' normal uniform allowances.

Six

Unsettling Times

Pictured here is the Manhattan Beach Traffic Bureau of 1981: (left to right) Sgts. John Wehner, Mike Carrs, Steve Fletcher, and Larry Munn.

The 1980s were a decade of complaints, suits, and general negativism, but the majority of the community thought the Police Department was doing an excellent job.

It was felt that officers were truly dedicated and professional when it came to enforcing state criminal statutes and traffic laws, exercising courtesy, and exhibiting friendliness when patrolling the city streets.

There was a great deal of controversy involving police budget cuts, and by mid-decade the town would be rocked by a no-confidence vote of new Chief Mertens. The McMartin Child Abuse case, as well as a bank president who assisted the IRS in the capture of a group of "grandmas" engaged in laundering drug money through a local bank, would make international news. It was a very unsettling time in the history of Manhattan Beach as well as in the Police Department.

In 1980, the residents of Manhattan Beach saw the first use of dogs in police work referred to as K-9 units. The canines were used for narcotics and arms detection. The first two dogs, shown here with their trainers, are Inga, with Officer Bob Bey, and Red, with Officer Frank DiBenedetto.

Officers who expressed interest in being a handler attended a 5-week basic training course at a local kennel and training center in Riverside, California. Handler and animal developed great respect and trust in each other, forming a bond that lasted throughout their careers. Red's retirement party was an emotional event for Officer Frank DiBenedetto in 1985.

Dogs have been used worldwide by law enforcement for many years, primarily due to their keen sense of smell. Most K-9 dogs are raised in European kennels. After an animal has been purchased and a handler has been selected, the new partners attend courses comprising extensive training in the search for suspects and evidence in both interior and exterior locations. With the completion of the course, the handler and dog become certified as a police patrol canine team. From this point on, training becomes a part of the team's daily activities and continues throughout the team's existence.

Law enforcement in 1982 was changing and Manhattan Beach Police changed with it. The pictured S.W.A.T. Team (Special Weapons and Tactical) prepares for the Los Angeles 1984 Olympic Games. The team is on duty 24 hours a day, every day of the year. From left to right are: (back row) Daniel Kuhn, Randolph Leaf, and Mike Matson; (front row) Bill Matson, Dale Reissig, and Berry Poppy (Fire Dept. Paramedic).

Qualifications for the K-9s to work on the SWAT team are much the same as their handlers; physical agility, strength, endurance tests, and daily training activities. The pride the handlers have in their relationship with the dogs can be seen in this photo. From left to right are Officers Frank DiBenedetto with Red, Bob Bey with Inga, and David Ferguson with Kai.

The team trained once a month either in the classroom or on the field. They are shown here in full battle dress. They train with MP-5 sub machine guns, Benelli shotguns, bean bag shotguns, AR-15 rifles, and pepperball and gas launchers. The K-9 dogs are also part of the team.

The pistol range was completed in September of 1970 at a cost of $31,000. The facility featured new concepts in sound reduction, lighting, and security. The department no longer had a pistol team, but firearm proficiency remained extremely important, keeping the pistol range in constant use.

Staff meetings are an everyday occurrence. Here the men in blue plan the day's agenda.

On Manhattan Beach Boulevard, one of the city's busiest streets, bicycle safety is a top priority. Here two young ladies are seen riding double, a serious safety violation that prompts the officers to intervene.

The apprehending officer impresses upon them the seriousness of their actions.

Thousands of people enjoy seaside recreation in Manhattan Beach during the summer months. The Beach Patrol Officers have a high visibility, keeping the peace and controlling the use of alcohol and drugs. The selected officers are equipped with a Nissan four-wheel drive pickup truck, affording better access across the entire beachfront.

Officers also use bicycles to patrol the bikepath, The Strand, and homes, looking out for possible burglaries or petty thefts. They have the same authority as an officer in a patrol car. As pictured here they are, from left to right: Andy Harrod, Mike Navarette, and Jim Ruiz.

Pressures of the job are removed with the relaxation and camaraderie of the game. From left to right are: (back row) Dino Caparelli, Lloyd Degonia, Tom Dalbec, Dave Ferguson, Bill Matson, Steve Fletcher, and Bob Bey; (front row) Harry Kuhlmeyer, Larry Munn, Bob Aciani, Bruce Powell, Frank DiBenedetto, and Bill Sapp.

The Chili Cook-Off at the City's "Hometown Fair" was a wonderful way for the Police Association to raise money. Pictured here in 1983, Officers Bob Bey and Steve Fletcher cook up a pot of their special Code-3 Chili (ladies unknown).

Patrol cars were better outfitted with more sophisticated equipment. Here Officer Micheal Navarette is using the Mobile Digital Terminal. The Manhattan Beach Police Force was the first department in the State of California to install these computers.

During the holiday season, Patrol Officer Dale Reissig exchanges greetings with the official band of the city, the Hyperion Outfall Serenaders.

On June 14, 1984, the Police and Fire Departments, City Council, and residents dedicated a Safety Officers' Memorial at the northeast corner of the police station. The flagpole stands at 25 feet and the Memorial Wall displays plaques inscribed with the names of those officers who have fallen in the line of duty.

Chief Ted Mertens, a 19-year police veteran, was introduced to the community on October 17, 1985. Many in the department resented the fact that he, like Chief Crumly, was not advanced from the ranks. Prior to being named the new chief, Mertens was chief of an 18-member police force in Placerville, California, a small town of about 7,500. The 14-year career of Chief Mertens in Manhattan Beach was a stormy one; many felt some of the friction was caused by city administration politics.

Volumes have been written about the McMartin child molestation case. The site of the alleged crimes took place here at the McMartin preschool and involved the elder Mrs. Buckey's son, Raymond Buckey, and several of the staff members. An arrest was made in August 1983 and would result in the longest investigation and trial in American criminal history. Located at the corner of Walnut Avenue and Manhattan Beach Boulevard, the preschool was owned by the Buckey family. The building was later razed.

"Believe the Children" was the main concern of these parents as they listened to Mr. John Cioffi, mayor of neighboring city Hermosa Beach. There were accusations about the handling of the case within the Manhattan Beach Police Department. Preliminary hearing for Mrs. Peggy McMartin Buckey lasted 18 months, the longest in California history. In August of 1990, the seven-year trial ended with all charges dropped against Raymond, who had spent five years in jail without being convicted. Many lives would never be the same.

In 1986, the Manhattan Beach Honor Guard had the privilege of being asked to Post the Colors at the 12th Annual Medal of Valor Luncheon.

That same year another hero, retired Brigadier General of the USAF, Charles (Chuck) E. Yeager, was the luncheon's keynote speaker for the day. He is photographed here with two ardent fans, Stacey and Scott Dennis.

The following year, 1987, Officers John Hensley and Randy Leaf showed extraordinary courage while on duty. It was a cold, windy night with high surf and rip tides when they responded to a frantic call for help. Stripping their gunbelts from their waists they plunged into the frigid waters in an attempt to rescue a woman caught in the surf. Their initial search being futile, they struggled back to shore only to be met by a screaming man pleading for them not to abandon the effort. The man then dove into the ocean, followed by Officer Hensley who got caught in the tide and was carried away. Firefighter John MacGregor arrived and together with Officer Leaf they swam out to save Hensley. Fortunately, both the woman and the man were found safe.

Safety Officers Andy Harrod and Hermosa Beach Officer Tommy Thompson bring current police information to the community by way of the *Community Awareness Program*, which airs on local TV.

In late 1982, Nigel Starkey, who had left London, England's, metropolitan police headquarters, was hired by Manhattan Beach's Police Chief Harry Kuhlmeyr. Starkey had been introduced to Manhattan Beach by officers who met him in England. Initially Detective Starkey was well-liked by the department as well as the community residents who met him.

That was all to change when on September 22, 1986, Officer Nigel Starkey was arrested on suspicion of raping a 23-year old female prisoner while she was incarcerated in the Manhattan Beach jail. The charges against him followed several weeks of investigation by a Special Task Force of the district attorney's office, which found enough evidence to prove guilt beyond a reasonable doubt.

Starkey was charged on October 10 and arraignment was set for February 10, 1987. On November 10th Starkey resigned from the Manhattan Beach Police Department. With the forfeiture of his British passport Starkey was freed on $20,000 bail. In a hearing before the judge in April of 1987, former Detective Starkey pleaded no contest to the charges of unlawful sexual behavior. He did not serve any jail time, but did leave the United States for a period of time.

In late January of 1987, Starkey (middle) his attorney, John Cheroske (left), and Officer Bob Bey of the Manhattan Beach Police force (right), leave the court room after Starkey was bound over for trial.

Contract negotiations with the city found the 49-member Police Association frustrated and angry. There had also been a no-confidence vote against Police Chief Ted Mertens. The issues were over both pay and benefits. On September 20, 1988, more then two dozen members picketed outside City Hall as council members and city staff arrived for a City Council meeting. The "angry blue line" announced a wide-ranging job action including no ticket writing.

Police still working without a contract set up a booth at the Hometown Fair to gain community support and hand out information.

Promotional posters were being produced to put across a positive profile of the men and women law enforcers, along with slogans such as "A Few Good People." This poster featured Sgt. Dale E. Reissig, Officer Patricia L. Picker (first woman patrol officer), and Officer Jamie D. Ruiz.

This is part of another poster representing the law enforcement divisions. In the back row are, from left to right: Officer Jim Noble, David C. Mullins, Steve Ohse, Sgt. John M. Milligan, and Daniel P. Kuhn; (front row) Officer David R. Ferguson with K-9 Kai.

Seven

STILL FOUR SQUARE MILES

In 1990 the Police Department had a budget of $7,006,470, which was 21.9 percent of the city's appropriations. Like much of the nation, the police department saw an increase in armed robberies, gang activity, and home burglary, as well as the need to create a special narcotics investigation team. While the use of illicit drugs had always been a concern of the department, the rise in substance abuse prompted a need to reevaluate efforts in this area. Two additional police officers were given training in the specialty assignments of narcotics and vice enforcement.

A regional task force, The West Side Narcotic Enforcement Team (WESTNET), made up of seven local communities in the South Bay, was in place and operational. Pictured here, officers display an enormous amount of cash ($21,000,000) and cocaine seized from a home in Sylmar, California. The suitcase alone contained $1,000,000. Kneeling in the foreground are Manhattan Officers Ed Medlock on the left and Frank DiBenedetto on the right.

In 1991 at the Medal of Valor and Distinguished Service Awards, approximately 600 people, including police officers and business leaders, honored 11 officers from around the South Bay. Three officers from Manhattan Beach were cited for their heroism: (center back row) Officers Daniel Kuhn, (back row right) Vincent Delmonico, and Gustavo Valdes.

Officers receiving promotions in 1991 are pictured from left to right: Capt. Robert Cashion, Lt. Dale Reisg, Sgt. John Dye, Sgt. Andrew Harrod, and Lt. Karl Nilsson. Chief Ted Mertens on the far right congratulated the officers.

Working undercover with the Los Angles Impact Team was a job that Frank DiBenedetto truly enjoyed. He spent 3 1/2 years tracking drug traffickers. In 1989 he was involved with the largest seizure of illegal steroids in California, and in 1990 the team confiscated half a ton of cocaine out of a semi-tractor trailer in Barstow, California. DiBenedetto has since retired from the force.

The Motor officers are part of the Traffic Bureau. The main purpose of these officers is their commitment to "providing traffic safety for the community." They are highly trained in radar/ laser speed detection and traffic collision investigation. At the time of this publication there are only three officers riding motorcycles.

Martin L. Ganz joined the Manhattan Beach police force in 1989 as a motorcycle officer. On December 27, 1993, he was shot down while making a routine traffic stop. At the age of 29, he was the second Manhattan Beach Police Officer killed in the line of duty. He will be remembered for his love of working with the school children and his interest and skill working in the DUI (Driving Under the Influence) enforcement program within the traffic division.

On January 3, 1994, City Mayor Steve Napolitano was among the 4,000 mourners who paid their respect to fallen officer Ganz.

Motorcycle officers salute as the pallbearers carry Ganz's casket to the grave site. The loss of Officer Ganz was deeply felt throughout the department.

In the Manhattan Beach Shopping Mall where the fatal shot took the life of Officer Ganz, a memorial plaque was placed at the site.

At the police station with appropriate ceremony a wall plaque was dedicated to the late Officer Martin Ganz. From left to right are Sgt. Mike Milligan, Officer Mark Mason, and Sgt. Dave Ferguson, with Chief Ted Mertens standing further to the right.

A composite drawing was instrumental in catching 28-year-old Roger Hoan Brady, who was identified by a witness as the suspected killer of Officer Ganz. After an eight-month manhunt, Brady was charged with robbery and murder in Oregon before facing charges in the Manhattan Beach death of Officer Ganz. After the trial it was recommended that Brady be put to death for the 1993 slaying of Officer Ganz.

For some time there had been discussion regarding the re-design of the police officers' star-shaped badge. As a kind of commemoration of Officer Ganz's death the star was changed to the shield photographed here.

Despite mounting friction within the department between officers and management, officers continued to do their job with dedication and professionalism. On March 31, 1994, responding to a possible car burglary in El Porto, officers blocked Highland Avenue for approximately one hour while searching for an auto burglary suspect.

In September of 1994, for the third time, Police chief Mertens received a vote of "no confidence" from the Police Officers Association (41 out of 49). They wanted him terminated! However, there were two sides to the controversy as the City Council responded with a unanimous vote of support for the Chief.

Mertens did acknowledge that there had been lingering animosities in the department since he was hired in 1987. Chief Mertens would retire in May of 1999.

William Ellis acted as interim police chief for five months until a new chief was hired in that same year.

Aside from the frictions of internal affairs, officers in the department have always been committed and dedicated to the community. In 1994, Crime Prevention Officer Stephanie Deason Martin, a veteran of 14 years on the force, received the Community Citizen of the Year award from the Lions Club. Pictured from left to right are Capt. Bob Cashion; Robert Smith, Lions Club President; Officer Stephanie Deason; Capt. John Hensley; and Mayor Steve Napolitano. Officer Martin is currently serving as a full-time school resource officer at Mira Costa High School.

One of the most decorated members of the force was Alk, a 7-1/2 year old German Shepherd police dog seen here with his trainer Mike Navarette. In the 1992 Inland Valley trials in San Bernardino he won first place and has received awards for his work in other canine competitions.

When suspicious packages are found, it is the Los Angeles Sheriff's Bomb Squad that is called by the Manhattan Beach police. Shown here is the arrival of the explosive shielding truck answering to a restaurant owner's discovery of a box looking like it might contain an explosive device. Fortunately the object was a hoax, but the efficient response was reassuring.

The highest honor possible for a police officer in the South Bay is the Medal of Valor Award. On April 23, 1998, Officer Gus Valdes and Karl Nilsson received the award in recognition of their pursuit of four armed robbers. While chasing the armed suspects on foot lethal shots were being fired. Due to the officers courageous efforts the four career criminals were successfully captured.

Manhattan Beach Crime prevention officer Gregg McMullin, along with other South Bay officers, appears on the local cable program, *Beach Beat* to discuss current crime in the South Bay cities.

Officer Jeanette Barker Meers has the distinction of being the first and only female to take part in the Manhattan Beach motorcycle traffic unit referred to as the Motor Team. She has been with the department for over ten years, spending four years riding in the traffic division. Officer Meers has additionally served on the SWAT Team and also has the designation of Crime Prevention Officer.

The Manhattan Beach Police Officers Association instituted an awards program in 1980 as a way to recognize outstanding officers. It was Detective Michael Rosenberger who was selected as "1998 Officer of the Year." He was considered an invaluable asset to the department. As a member of the SWAT Team he functioned as a field training officer, fire instructor, and drug training officer. As a certified computer crimes investigator he was able to assist in the investigation of crimes that occur via the Internet.

By the end of 1999, the number of DUI violations in Manhattan Beach was at a seven-year low. The increase in the amount of fines, well-trained officers in the testing of motorists suspected of driving under the influence, and a decrease in the habituation of local bars were major factors in the decline.

Retirement celebrations were always marked with good fellowship and lighthearted fun. Many of the events were announced with cleverly-crafted posters such as the four following samples. This one announced the double retirement of Officers Gene Guitare and Jack Dutchess.

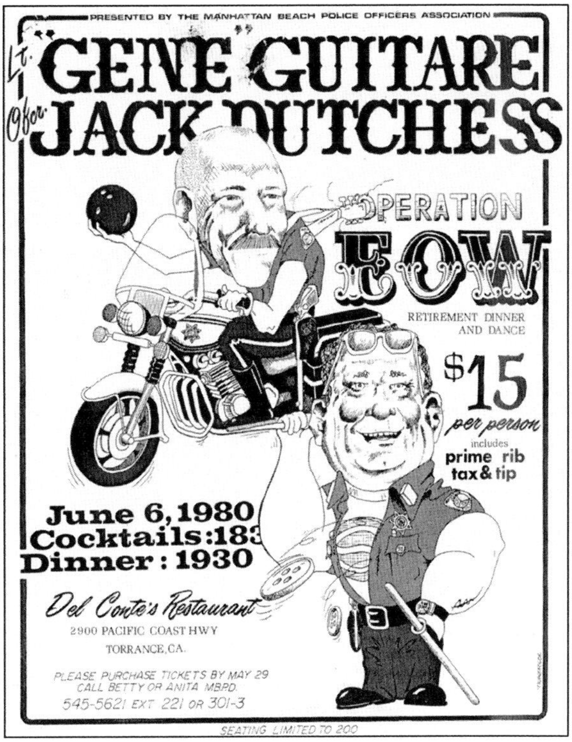

For his length and dedication of service, Officer Don Stone was considered a legend in his own time.

Police Chief Harry Kuhlmeyer bade farewell in 1985.

Lieutenant Bruce Powell's 35 years marked a service record longer than any other officer.

On July 19, 1999, Ernest Klevesahl became the city's eleventh Police Chief. Klevesahl, who prefers to be called "Chief Ernie," entered the office from Grover Beach, California, a community three times smaller than Manhattan Beach. There he served as director of the Police and Fire Department working with a budget of only $2.1 million, as compared to $10.8 million appropriated for Manhattan Beach. Clearly the challenges were going to be greater. As a 25-year veteran in law enforcement he previously served 20 years of that with the San Diego Sheriff's Department as a sergeant and lieutenant.

Though the community was still four square miles, the make-up of its population and visitors was rapidly changing. So, too, were police methods and technical equipment. The department recognized the need to install video cameras and wireless microphones in their patrol cars. Public awareness of the modernization made some fear "Big Brotherism," yet in fact such devices had long been installed within the station and jail area since 1997.

Bank robberies, many turning violent, have been on a steady increase in Manhattan Beach. No longer is the city the small isolated community it was in 1922 boasting but one bank. Statistic show bank robberies have escalated from 36 in 2000 to 53 in 2001.

On November 11, 1999, the Manhattan Beach Police Department had a new lieutenant when Sergeant Derrick Abell, a nine-year veteran of the force, was promoted. Abell is the first African American lieutenant in the department's history. He has served in many capacities in the department, some of which are patrol and overseeing the canine and D.A.R.E. programs. Lieutenant Abell also is a member of the SWAT Team.

In an effort to reduce the number of traffic accidents in the city, a Stopper Traffic Safety Awareness Campaign was put into operation. With the slogan "Do Stop. Don't Speed." it has become an effective program that has significantly contributed to a drop in traffic violations. Shown in the photo, the costumed Stopper character appears with a group of school children.

There are Victims' Assistance Teams throughout the United States, which have been recognized by the International Association of Police Chiefs in Washington D.C. The Manhattan Beach's team responds 24 hours a day to help victims of crime. Working closely with the police department, they are, from left to right: (front row) Gayle Wilhite, coordinator Sandy Taylor, and Phyllis Barreric; (back row) Mary Golob, Jeannette Wright, Sherrell Paric, Stewart Fournir, Lisa Meadows, Janc Bateman, and Landy Oaker.

The Police Department assists in many traffic control activities within the community. The Manhattan Beach 10K run is one such event. Police Chief Ernest Klevesahl and Sgt. Andy Harrod receive a framed T-shirt from committee members Anne Caplan and Carol Champagne.

In 2001, Chief "Ernie" was instrumental in the development of the "Community Police Academy." The goals of the project were to make the community more aware of the department's functions and to enhance communication between the police and the residents. Officers associated with various divisions within the force conduct the classes. Law enforcement personnel guided the first graduates through a ten-week program. Seated from left to right are Sergeant Nan Rados, 16 years with the department; Chief Klevesahl; Officer Tim Hageman, who has been with the department since 1991; and Jennifer Street.

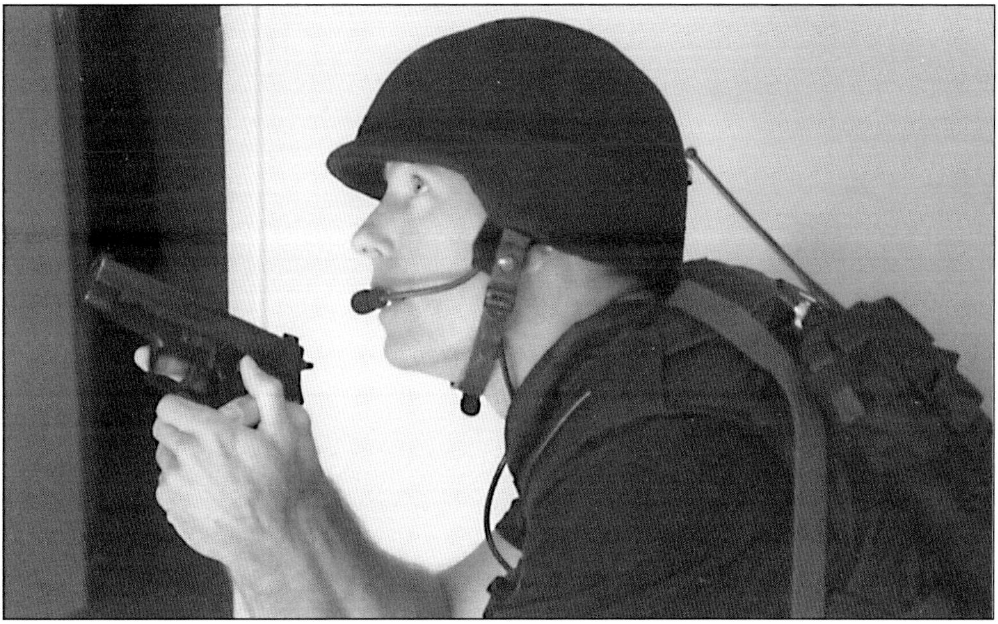

Keeping fit is a prime qualification for the SWAT team. An officer has to have worked for the Manhattan Beach Police Department for a minimum of one year, successfully completed the physical agility, strength, and endurance tests, and performed an evaluation and oral interview with SWAT Commanders.

A new Police/Fire Safety facility has been a dream of the departments for many years. Both the police and fire stations are too small and outdated for the current public safety employees. The new $35,000,000 facility will be built at the present location of the Police/Fire stations, 15th Street and Valley Drive. The new public safety building will meet the needs of departments' space, comply with earthquake safety standards, provide greater parking for department equipment, and provide storage for supplies. The police facility will accommodate a five-lane firing range and a separate interactive electronic range, a nine-cell jail, seven holding cells, and two sobering cells. Dormitories for firefighters are also in the plans. A few years will be required before this much-needed 54,503-square-foot facility can be operational.

Officer Joey Guzman and Nero the German Shepherd today make up the K-9 Team. Officer Guzman served as a reserve officer and police cadet in the community before being hired by the Manhattan Beach police Department in 1994. Officer Guzman has been Nero's handler for three years. Nero was born in the Czech Republic and responds only to Czech commands. The team has been in patrol and narcotics detection by the State of California.

Over the last 90 years, hundreds of officers have served in the Manhattan Beach Police Department. Officer Steven Fletcher, who spent 31 years in the department, 27 of which had been spent riding motorcycles, is but one of those dedicated officers. We salute you ALL.

A Policeman's Prayer

Dear Lord, be with me on my beat
This day and every day.
Grant that each weary block I walk
May ease a brother's way.
Let me be kindly to the old
And to the young be strong,
But let me triumph over those
Whose acts are cruel or wrong.
And when my own last summons comes
And I stand in Your Court,
Lord, may my rest with You be long,
My punishment be short.

This is a Policeman's Prayer.